# Comfy O'Charley's Copycat Recipes

Delicious Everyday Meals for You

## BY: Martin Beasant

Reserved Rights and Copyright © 2024, Martin Beasant.

# Notification Page

Hello there,

I kindly request that you refrain from reproducing this book in any form, whether it be printed or electronic, sold, published, disseminated or distributed without obtaining prior written permission from the author.

I have taken great care in ensuring that the content of this book is accurate and helpful, but it is the reader's responsibility to exercise caution in their actions. Please note that the author cannot be held responsible for any consequences resulting from the reader's actions.

Thank you for your understanding and cooperation.


Sincerely,

Martin Beasant

# Table of Contents

Introduction .................................................................................................... 5

1. California Salad ....................................................................................... 6

2. Barbecue Chicken ................................................................................... 9

3. Shrimp Scampi ...................................................................................... 11

4. French Dip Sandwich ............................................................................ 13

5. Three Cheese Shrimp Dip ..................................................................... 15

6. Chicken Tenders .................................................................................... 17

7. Honey Mustard ...................................................................................... 19

8. Loaded Potato Soup .............................................................................. 21

9. Harvest Soup ......................................................................................... 23

10. Chicken Caesar Salad ......................................................................... 25

11. Chicken Pot Pie ................................................................................... 27

12. Loaded Cheese Fries ........................................................................... 30

13. Blackened Salmon ............................................................................... 32

14. BBQ Ribs ............................................................................................ 34

15. Broccoli Cheese Casserole .................................................................. 36

16. Honey Mustard Chicken .................................................................... 38

17. Prime Rib ........................................................................................... 40

18. Baked Potato ...................................................................................... 42

19. Pecan Chicken Tender Salad ............................................................ 44

20. Southern Fried Chicken .................................................................... 46

21. Chicken Tortilla Soup ....................................................................... 48

22. Cajun Shrimp Pasta ........................................................................... 51

23. Baked Penne Italiano ........................................................................ 53

24. Beer Battered Onion Rings ............................................................... 56

25. Dinner Rolls ....................................................................................... 58

26. Cinnamon Sugar Donuts ................................................................... 60

27. Key Lime Pie ..................................................................................... 62

28. Strawberry Lemonade ....................................................................... 64

29. Chocolate Chip Cookie Skillet ......................................................... 66

30. Caramel Pie ........................................................................................ 68

Conclusion .................................................................................................. 70

Dear Reader ................................................................................................ 71

# Introduction

Enjoy restaurant-style meals in the comfort of your home, budget, and effort. The meals shared here, which are inspired by O'Charley's meals, give you many reasons to eat well and deliciously.

It features salads, soups, pies, dips, full meals, and desserts for flexibility in your meal plan. They are also perfect for family servings and batch cooking.

Make a hearty pot of potato soup gourmet style while using affordable ingredients. And while at it, feel free to tweak things up for your personalization. This and many more meals await you ahead.

# 1. California Salad

A fruity salad with grilled chicken, nuts, and tasty balsamic dressing.

**Prep Time: 10 mins**

**Serves: 4**

**Ingredients:**

**Balsamic dressing:**

- 1 tbsp mayonnaise
- ¼ cup balsamic vinegar
- ½ cup olive oil
- 1 tsp dark or light brown sugar
- 1 tbsp minced garlic
- ½ tsp salt or to taste
- ½ tsp black pepper

**Salad:**

- 3 cups chopped romaine lettuce
- 2 cups chopped grilled chicken
- ½ cup strawberries, sliced
- ½ cup mandarin oranges
- ¼ cup dried cranberries
- ⅓ cup blue cheese crumbles
- ⅓ cup candied pecans

**Instructions:**

**For the balsamic dressing:**

Whisk the vinaigrette ingredients in a bowl until smooth.

**For the salad:**

Place the lettuce in a large bowl and distribute the remaining ingredients on top. Serve with the dressing.

# 2. Barbecue Chicken

Simple, barbecue chicken with great flavor and ready in 30 minutes.

**Prep Time: 10 mins**

**Cook Time: 30 mins**

**Serves: 16**

**Ingredients:**

- 1 tbsp paprika
- 1 tbsp brown sugar
- 1 tsp garlic powder
- 1 tsp ground cumin
- 1 tsp dry mustard
- 1 tsp onion powder
- ¼ tsp cayenne pepper
- 1 ½ cups sweet barbecue sauce
- Salt and black pepper to taste
- 4 lb. chicken drumsticks

**Instructions:**

Preheat the oven to 425°F. Line a baking sheet with foil. Set it aside.

Mix all the ingredients in a large bowl except for the chicken. Pat the chicken dry and coat it with the sauce, saving some for basting.

Arrange the chicken on the baking sheet and bake for 30 minutes or until cooked through, reaching an internal temperature of 165°F. Baste the chicken with the remaining sauce while baking.

# 3. Shrimp Scampi

Authentic and tasty shrimp scampi with the right tang and heat to it.

**Prep Time: 10 mins**

**Cook Time: 20 mins**

**Serves: 4**

**Ingredients:**

- 1 lb. linguine
- ½ cup unsalted butter
- 2 tbsp minced garlic
- ½ tsp salt
- ½ tsp black pepper
- 1 lb. large shrimp, peeled and deveined, with tails on
- ⅓ cup dry white wine
- ¼ tsp red pepper flakes
- 2 tbsp chopped fresh parsley
- ½ lemon, juiced

**Instructions:**

Cook the linguine according to the package's instructions. Drain well when ready.

Meanwhile, melt the butter in a large skillet over medium heat and sauté the garlic, salt, and black pepper for 1 minute or until fragrant.

Add the shrimp and cook for 1 to 2 minutes or until no longer pink. Put the shrimp on a plate.

Deglaze the pan with the wine and cook until reduced by half and slightly thickened. Stir through the red pepper flakes, parsley, and lemon juice. Add the pasta and toss to coat well. Toss the shrimp through.

Serve immediately.

# 4. French Dip Sandwich

A mouth-wetting sandwich packed with beef, onion, and provolone cheese.

**Prep Time: 10 mins**

**Cook Time: 4 hours**

**Serves: 4**

**Ingredients:**

- 1 (3 to 4 lb.) beef chuck roast
- 1 onion, sliced
- 4 cloves garlic, minced
- 4 cups beef broth
- 1 tsp salt
- ½ tsp black pepper
- 4 hoagie rolls
- 8 slices provolone cheese

**Instructions:**

Put the ingredients in a slow cooker except for the rolls and cheese. Cover and cook on HIGH for 4 hours or until the beef is tender and easily falls apart.

Transfer the beef to a plate and shred it with 2 forks. Return the beef to the cooker and stir through with the sauce.

Toast the rolls in the broiler or a skillet.

Fill the rolls with cheese, beef, and onion. Serve warm with the cooking juice for dipping.

# 5. Three Cheese Shrimp Dip

A delicious cheesy appetizer or snack with speckles of shrimp scattered all through.

**Prep Time: 10 mins**

**Cook Time: 25 mins**

**Serves: 4+**

**Ingredients:**

- 1 (6 oz) can small shrimp
- ½ cup Parmesan, Romano, and asiago cheese blend
- 1 tsp Old Bay Seasoning or to taste
- ½ tsp onion powder or to taste
- ½ tsp garlic powder or to taste
- 8 oz cream cheese, softened
- 1 (14.5 oz) can diced tomatoes, fully drained
- 6 oz shredded Monterey Jack cheese
- 6 oz shredded mild cheddar cheese
- Tortilla chips or crusty bread for serving

**Instructions:**

Preheat the oven to 325°F. Grease a casserole dish with cooking spray. Set it aside.

Mix all the ingredients except the Monterey Jack, cheddar cheese, and tortilla chips or crusty bread. Spread the mixture in the casserole dish. Bake uncovered for 20 minutes or until the top starts to brown.

Sprinkle the remaining cheese on top and bake until the cheese is bubbly.

Serve warm with tortilla chips or crusty bread.

# 6. Chicken Tenders

Crispy chicken with delicious seasoning for snacking, light lunch, or salads.

**Prep Time: 10 mins**

**Cook Time: 10 mins**

**Serves: 4**

**Ingredients:**

- 1 lb. chicken tenders
- 1 cup all-purpose flour
- 1 tsp paprika
- 1 tsp garlic powder
- 1 tsp dried thyme
- 1 tsp salt
- ½ tsp black pepper
- 2 eggs
- ¼ cup milk
- Vegetable oil, for frying

**Instructions:**

Preheat the oven to 200°F.

Mix the flour and seasonings in a shallow bowl. Crack the eggs into a separate bowl and beat with the milk.

Dredge the chicken in the flour mixture until well coated, dip in the eggs, and in the flour mixture again.

Heat ¼-inch of oil in a deep skillet to 375°F. Fry the chicken in batches for 3 to 5 minutes per side or until they are golden brown and cooked through. Drain on paper towels.

Serve with the sauce.

# 7. Honey Mustard

This sweet and tangy dressing is perfect for a wide range of salads.

**Prep Time: 5 mins**

**Serves: 4**

**Ingredients:**

- 1 cup mayonnaise
- ½ cup yellow mustard
- 2 tsp apple cider vinegar
- ½ cup honey
- 2 tbsp poppy seeds
- ½ tsp salt

**Instructions:**

Mix all the ingredients in a bowl until well combined. Serve.

# 8. Loaded Potato Soup

Simply loaded with potatoes, bacon, and cheddar. Throw on some green onions for extra crunch.

**Prep Time: 15 mins**

**Cook Time: 40 mins**

**Serves: 4**

**Ingredients:**

- 4 slices bacon, diced
- 5 medium potatoes, peeled and cubed
- ½ onion, chopped
- 3 cloves garlic, minced
- 4 cups chicken broth
- 1 cup heavy cream
- ½ cup of shredded cheddar cheese
- Salt and black pepper to taste

**Instructions:**

Cook the bacon in a large pot over medium heat until crispy. Remove the bacon and drain it on paper towels.

Sauté the onion and garlic in the same pot for 2 to 3 minutes or until tender. Add the potatoes and chicken broth. Boil and simmer over reduced heat for 20 minutes or until the potatoes are tender.

Mash some of the potatoes to thicken the soup and stir through the heavy cream. Simmer for 1 to 2 more minutes.

Stir through the bacon, cheese, salt, and black pepper. Serve hot.

# 9. Harvest Soup

Delicious broth packed with tender egg noodles, chunky soft veggies, and chicken.

**Prep Time: 10 mins**

**Cook Time: 40 mins**

**Serves: 4**

**Ingredients:**

- ¼ lb. butter
- ¾ cup flour
- 2 ½ quarts water
- 2 tbsp chicken base
- 2 quarts chicken stock
- 1 lb. fresh carrots, diced
- 1 medium onion, diced
- 7 ribs celery, diced
- ¾ tsp garlic powder
- ¾ tsp white pepper
- 10 oz egg noodles
- 5 cups chopped cooked chicken tenders

**Instructions:**

Melt the butter in a large pot over medium heat and mix in the flour until well combined. Cook for 2 to 3 minutes. Slowly stir the water through until smooth. Simmer over reduced heat for 20 minutes. Stir through the chicken stock and chicken base. Add the carrots, onion, and celery. Cook for 6 minutes or until tender.

Stir through the garlic powder, white pepper, and noodles. Cook for 3 to 4 minutes or until the egg noodles are tender. Stir the chicken through and heat through for 2 to 3 minutes.

Serve warm.

# 10. Chicken Caesar Salad

A good way to revamp leftover grilled chicken in this fresh Caesar salad.

**Prep Time: 15 mins**

**Serves: 4**

**Ingredients:**

- 1 head of romaine lettuce, chopped
- ½ cup Caesar dressing
- 2 grilled chicken breasts, sliced into strips
- 1 cup croutons
- 1 cup grated Parmesan cheese
- Salt and black pepper to taste

**Instructions:**

Toss the romaine lettuce with the Caesar dressing in a large bowl. Top with the chicken, croutons, and Parmesan cheese. Serve immediately.

# 11. Chicken Pot Pie

Savory pie with an appetizing golden crust and filled with tender chicken, pearl onions, peas, carrots, and a rich sauce.

**Prep Time: 15 mins**

**Cook Time: 50 mins**

**Serves: 4**

**Ingredients:**

- 1 tbsp olive oil
- 1 lb. boneless, skinless chicken breast, cubed
- Salt and black pepper to taste
- ¼ cup unsalted butter
- ¼ cup all-purpose flour
- 1 cup chicken broth
- 1 cup milk
- ½ tsp dried thyme
- 1 cup frozen carrots and peas
- ½ cup frozen pearl onions
- 1 store-bought pie crust

**Instructions:**

Preheat the oven to 375°F.

Heat a large skillet with olive oil over medium heat. Season the chicken with salt and black pepper; cook for 4 to 5 minutes per side or until browned and cooked through. Remove the chicken onto a plate. Let rest for 5 minutes, and chop it into small pieces.

Melt the butter in the same skillet and stir through the flour. Cook for 1 minute. Gradually stir in the chicken broth and milk until smooth. Cook until bubbly and thickened. Season with salt, black pepper, and thyme. Stir in the carrots and peas, pearl onions, and chicken.

Pour the mixture into a deep-dish pie plate. Roll out the pie crust on a lightly floured surface and lay it over the pie dish. Trim and crimp the edges and cut slits at the center of the crust for ventilation.

Bake for 45 to 50 minutes or until the crust is golden and the filling is bubbly. Cool for a few minutes before serving.

# 12. Loaded Cheese Fries

A splurgy platter loaded with potatoes, cheese, bacon, and aromatic parsley.

**Prep Time: 20 mins**

**Cook Time: 30 mins**

**Serves: 4**

**Ingredients:**

- 4 large Russet potatoes
- Olive oil for drizzling
- Salt and black pepper to taste
- 2 cups shredded cheddar cheese
- 6 slices bacon, cooked and crumbled
- ½ cup ranch dressing
- Chopped parsley, for garnish

**Instructions:**

Preheat the oven to 400°F.

Cut the potatoes into thin sticks and spread them on a baking sheet. Drizzle with olive oil and season with salt and black pepper. Roast for 20 to 25 minutes or until golden and crispy.

Sprinkle cheese over the fried and bake for 5 more minutes or until the cheese melts.

Take out of the oven, sprinkle with bacon, and drizzle with the ranch dressing. Garnish with parsley before serving.

# 13. Blackened Salmon

Spicy smoky Cajun salmon cooked to perfection.

**Prep Time: 10 mins**

**Cook Time: 20 mins**

**Serves: 4**

**Ingredients:**

- 4 (6 oz) salmon fillets
- 2 tbsp olive oil
- 2 tbsp Cajun seasoning
- 1 tsp smoked paprika
- ½ tsp garlic powder
- ½ tsp onion powder
- Salt and black pepper to taste

**Instructions:**

Preheat the oven to 400°F. Line a baking sheet with parchment paper.

Mix the seasonings in a bowl. Brush the salmon with olive oil and rub the seasoning all over the filets.

Heat a skillet over medium heat and lay the salmon skin-side down. Cook for 2 to 3 minutes per side. Transfer the salmon to the baking sheet and bake for 10 to 12 minutes or until the fish starts to easily flake with a fork.

Serve the salmon immediately.

# 14. BBQ Ribs

Classic BBQ ribs that are pre-seasoned with a sweet spicy rub and dressed with BBQ sauce. They are also slow-cooked for meat that easily falls off the bones.

**Prep Time: 10 mins**

**Cook Time: 3 hours**

**Serves: 4**

**Ingredients:**

- ½ cup brown sugar
- 1 tbsp onion powder
- 1 tbsp garlic powder
- 1 tbsp chili powder
- ¼ cup paprika
- 1 tbsp cumin
- Salt and black pepper to taste
- 2 racks baby back pork ribs
- 1 cup BBQ sauce

**Instructions:**

Preheat the oven to 275°F.

Mix the seasonings in a bowl. Pat dry the ribs with paper towels and rub the seasoning mix all over it. Place the ribs on the baking sheet and bake for 2 ½ to 3 hours or until tender.

Baste the ribs on both sides with the BBQ sauce and bake for 10 more minutes. Let it rest for 10 minutes before slicing and serving.

# 15. Broccoli Cheese Casserole

A fun and yummy way to enjoy broccoli. Drenched in a creamy, cheesy sauce, and baked perfectly with a golden reveal on top.

**Prep Time: 10 mins**

**Cook Time: 37 mins**

**Serves: 4**

**Ingredients:**

- 4 cups broccoli florets
- ¼ cup unsalted butter
- ¼ cup all-purpose flour
- 2 cups milk
- Salt and black pepper to taste
- 1 cup grated cheddar cheese
- ½ cup panko breadcrumbs

**Instructions:**

Preheat the oven to 375°F.

Steam the broccoli florets for 5 minutes or until they are crisp-tender.

Melt the butter in a saucepan over medium heat. Next, whisk in the flour until smooth and cook for 1 to 2 minutes. Gradually stir through the milk until smooth and thick. Season with salt and black pepper. Stir the cheese through until melted. Fold in the steamed broccoli until well coated.

Pour the mixture into a baking dish, sprinkle the breadcrumbs on top, and bake for 25 to 30 minutes or until golden and bubbly.

Serve warm.

# 16. Honey Mustard Chicken

Sweet, tangy, and yummy chicken perfect for serving with greens and potatoes.

**Prep Time: 10 mins**

**Cook Time: 24 mins**

**Serves: 4**

**Ingredients:**

- 4 chicken breasts, boneless and skinless
- Salt and black pepper, to taste
- 1 tsp garlic powder
- 1 tbsp olive oil
- ¼ cup yellow mustard
- ¼ cup Dijon mustard
- ½ cup honey
- 1 tbsp apple cider vinegar

**Instructions:**

Preheat the oven to 375°F.

Season the chicken with salt, black pepper, and garlic powder.

Heat a large skillet with olive oil over medium heat. Sear the chicken for 1 to 2 minutes per side or until golden brown. Place the chicken in a baking dish.

Mix the remaining ingredients in a bowl and pour it over the chicken. Bake for 15 to 20 minutes or until reaches an internal temperature of 165°F.

Serve the chicken warm.

# 17. Prime Rib

A classic rib roast well-herbed and exploding with satisfying flavors.

**Prep Time: 20 mins**

**Cook Time: 2 ½ hours**

**Serves: 8+**

**Ingredients:**

- 4 garlic cloves, minced
- 2 tbsp chopped fresh thyme
- 2 tbsp chopped fresh rosemary
- 2 tbsp kosher salt
- 2 tsp black pepper
- 2 tbsp olive oil
- 4 lb. prime rib roast

**Instructions:**

Preheat the oven to 450°F.

Mix the ingredients in a bowl except for the prime rib roast. Pat dry the meat with paper towels and brush the seasoning mixture all over it. Place the meat on a roasting pan.

Roast for 20 minutes. Reduce the oven's temperature to 325°F and roast for 2 to 2 ½ hours more or until it reaches your desired doneness.

Let it rest out of the oven for 10 minutes before slicing and serving.

# 18. Baked Potato

Tenderly baked potatoes with a mouthwatering filling of butter, sour cream, cheese, and bacon. Throw on some chopped green onions for extra character and crunch.

**Prep Time: 15 mins**

**Cook Time: 1 hour**

**Serves: 4**

**Ingredients:**

- 4 large baking potatoes, well-scrubbed and patted dry
- ¼ cup unsalted butter
- ¼ cup sour cream
- ¼ cup shredded cheddar cheese
- 4 strips of cooked bacon, crumbled
- Salt and black pepper to taste

**Instructions:**

Preheat the oven to 375°F.

Rub the potatoes with a bit of butter and salt. Pierce the potatoes with a fork all around. Place the potatoes on a baking sheet and bake for 1 hour or until they are tender and cooked through. Cool the potatoes for a few minutes or until handleable.

Cut the potatoes vertically in half and use a fork to fluff the potatoes within its shell.

For each potato, top with a tbsp of butter, sour cream, cheese, and bacon. Season with salt and black pepper. Serve immediately.

# 19. Pecan Chicken Tender Salad

Throw some cranberries into this chicken-crunchy salad to elevate its look, taste, and character.

**Prep Time: 15 mins**

**Cook Time: 15 mins**

**Serves: 4**

**Ingredients:**

- 2 cups panko breadcrumbs
- ¼ cup grated Parmesan cheese
- 1 lb. chicken tenders
- 1 cup flour
- 2 eggs, beaten
- Salt and black pepper
- 4 cups mixed greens
- ½ cup grape tomatoes
- ½ red onion, sliced
- ½ cup chopped pecans
- ¼ cup honey mustard dressing (see honey mustard recipe)

**Instructions:**

Preheat the oven to 375°F.

Mix the breadcrumbs with the Parmesan cheese on a shallow plate. Dredge the chicken tenders in flour, dip them in the eggs, and coat them in the Parmesan mixture, pressing to adhere the coating well. Place the chicken on a baking sheet and bake for 15 minutes or until golden brown.

Mix the greens, tomatoes, red onion, and pecans in a large bowl. Top with the chicken and drizzle on the dressing. Serve.

# 20. Southern Fried Chicken

Crunchy flavourful chicken with a scrumptious Southern touch to it.

**Prep Time: 15 mins**

**Cook Time: 45 mins**

**Serves: 4**

**Ingredients:**

- Vegetable oil for frying
- 1 cup all-purpose flour
- 1 tbsp garlic powder
- 1 tsp cayenne pepper
- 1 tbsp paprika
- 1 tsp salt
- 1 tsp black pepper
- 1 tbsp onion powder
- 4 bone-in chicken thighs
- ½ cup buttermilk

**Instructions:**

Heat 2 inches of oil in a deep skillet or heavy-bottomed pot over medium heat.

Mix the remaining ingredients in a shallow dish except for the buttermilk. Pour the buttermilk into another bowl.

Dredge the chicken in the flour mixture, dip them in the buttermilk, and coat it with the flour mixture again. Shake off any excess flour and fry the chicken for 10 to 12 minutes or until they reach an internal temperature of 165°F.

Drain the chicken on paper towels before serving.

# 21. Chicken Tortilla Soup

Tasty Mexican-style soup with good heat, yummy fillings, and toppings for a satisfying lunch.

**Prep Time: 15 mins**

**Cook Time: 95 mins**

**Serves: 6**

**Ingredients:**

- 4 large ripe red tomatoes, cored and quartered
- 1 large white onion, peeled and quartered
- 2 tbsp olive oil
- ¼ tsp sea salt
- 1 tsp dried oregano, preferably Mexican
- 1 dried pasilla chile
- 2 dried guajillo chiles
- 4 unpeeled garlic cloves
- Salt and white pepper to taste
- 2 cups corn kernels
- 3 medium zucchinis, diced
- 1 bunch cilantro, including stems, chopped
- Salt and black pepper to taste

**For topping:**

- 6 oz queso fresco, cubed
- 2 avocados, cubed
- 3 radishes, thinly sliced
- 2 tbsp cilantro leaves
- Corn tortilla chips
- Chopped fresh cilantro for garnish

**Instructions:**

Preheat the oven to 450°F.

Spread the tomatoes, onion, and unpeeled garlic on a baking sheet. Toss with the olive oil, salt, and oregano. Roast in the oven for 45 minutes or until the veggies are black around the edges, stirring every 15 minutes.

Toast the dry chilies in a skillet over medium heat for 1 minute and soak them in a bowl with boiling water for 30 minutes. Remove the chilies into a blender, reserving the liquid. Peel the garlic and add it to the blender along with the tomatoes, onions, and roasting juices. Add 2 cups of watering blend (including the chilies liquid) until smooth.

Strain the mixture into a pot, squeezing out as much liquid, and discard the solids. Add 4 cups of water to the broth, boil, and then simmer over reduced heat for 10 minutes.

Stir the corn, zucchini, cilantro, salt, and black pepper through. Cook for 10 more minutes or until the zucchini is crisp-tender. Serve the soup warm with the toppings.

# 22. Cajun Shrimp Pasta

Mouthwatering Cajun shrimp pasta with a delicious restaurant-style touch.

**Prep Time: 20 mins**

**Cook Time: 20 mins**

**Serves: 4**

**Ingredients:**

- 1 lb. angel hair pasta
- ¼ cup butter
- ½ cup coarsely chopped red bell pepper
- ½ cup coarsely chopped green pepper
- ½ cup coarsely chopped red onion
- 1 lb. shrimp, peeled and deveined
- 1 tbsp flour
- 2 ½ cups half and half
- Garlic powder to taste
- Salt and black pepper to taste
- Cajun seasoning to taste

**Instructions:**

Cook the angel hair pasta according to the package's instructions. Drain well and set it aside.

Meanwhile, melt the butter in a large skillet over medium heat. Sauté the onion and bell peppers for 3 minutes or until tender. Add the shrimp and cook for 2 to 3 minutes or until pink. Stir through the flour and then the half-and-half until smoothly combined. Season with salt, black pepper, garlic powder, and Cajun seasoning. Simmer for 1 minute.

Toss in the pasta until well coated with the sauce. Serve warm.

# 23. Baked Penne Italiano

Dinner is served with this creamy, meaty pasta dish. Well-seasoned and family-sized.

**Prep Time: 15 mins**

**Cook Time: 53 mins**

**Serves: 4**

**Ingredients:**

- 1 lb. penne pasta
- 3 tbsp extra virgin olive oil
- 2 cloves garlic, minced
- 1 lb. hot or sweet Italian fennel sausage, casings removed
- 1 (28 oz) can tomato puree
- 1 ½ tsp granulated sugar
- 1 ½ cups water
- ¼ tsp ground fennel
- 1 bay leaf
- Salt and black pepper to taste
- 3 cups creamy ricotta cheese
- ½ lb. fresh mozzarella cheese, cut into ½-inch cubes
- ¼ cup freshly grated Parmigiano-Reggiano cheese

**Instructions:**

Preheat the oven to 400°F.

Cook the pasta according to the package's instructions. Drain well.

Meanwhile, heat the olive oil in a large skillet over medium heat and sauté the garlic for 1 minute or until fragrant. Add the sausage and cook for 8 minutes or until browned, breaking up the meat while cooking. Stir through the tomato puree, sugar, water, fennel, bay leaf, salt, and black pepper. Boil and then simmer over reduced heat for 30 minutes. Discard the bay leaf.

Stir the creamy ricotta through and toss in the pasta until well coated. Pour the mixture into a baking dish and distribute the mozzarella and Parmigiano-Reggiano on top.

Bake for 45 minutes or until golden and bubbly. Rest for 20 minutes before serving.

# 24. Beer Battered Onion Rings

Crunchy golden onion rings as a tasty appetizer. Serve them with a wide range of dipping sauces.

**Prep Time: 20 mins**

**Chilling Time: 4 hours**

**Cook Time: 20 mins**

**Serves: 4**

**Ingredients:**

- 1 ⅓ cups all-purpose flour
- 1 tsp salt
- ¼ tsp black pepper to taste
- 1 tbsp vegetable oil
- 2 egg yolks
- ¾ cup good quality beer
- 2 large sweet onions, sliced into thick rings and separated
- Vegetable oil for frying

**Instructions:**

Mix the flour, salt, and black pepper in a shallow dish. Whisk in the egg yolks, 1 tbsp of vegetable oil, and beer until smooth. Cover the bowl and refrigerate for 3 to 4 hours.

Heat 2 inches of vegetable oil in a deep skillet over medium heat to 370°F.

In batches, dip the onion rings 3 to 4 times in the batter and fry in the oil until golden brown. Drain on paper towels.

Serve with your favorite dipping sauce.

# 25. Dinner Rolls

Sumptuous, fluffy, and warm rolls to pair with soups and more.

**Prep Time: 30 mins**

**Rising Time: 2 hours**

**Cook Time: 15 mins**

**Serves: 9**

**Ingredients:**

- ½ cup vegetable oil
- ½ cup boiling water
- ⅓ cup sugar
- 1 tsp salt
- ½ cup warm water
- 1 small package of dry yeast
- 1 large egg, beaten
- 3 cups flour, plus extra for dusting

**Instructions:**

Preheat the oven to 400. Grease a baking sheet with cooking spray and set it aside.

Mix the oil, boiling water, sugar, and salt in a bowl. Mix the warm water and yeast and stir it into the oil liquid. Whisk in the egg until smooth. Mix in the flour, lightly flour the mixture and form into a ball. Cover the bowl with a clean napkin and let it rise for 2 hours.

Lightly flour a surface and transfer the dough ball onto it. Divide the dough ball into 3 pieces and divide each ball into 3 pieces. Roll each piece into a ball. Arrange the dough balls on the baking sheet, cover them, and let them rise for 2 hours.

Bake for 10 to 15 minutes or until golden brown and puffed.

Serve warm.

# 26. Cinnamon Sugar Donuts

Sweet tooth satisfying, warm, and fluffy with a decadent coating of cinnamon sugar.

**Prep Time: 15 mins**

**Cook Time: 10 mins**

**Serves: 4**

**Ingredients:**

- 1 cup all-purpose flour
- 1 tbsp baking powder
- 1 ½ tsp ground cinnamon, divided
- ¼ cup + ½ cup granulated sugar, divided
- ½ cup milk
- 2 tbsp + ¼ cup unsalted butter, melted
- 1 egg, cracked into a bowl

**Instructions:**

Preheat the oven to 375°F. Grease a donut pan with cooking spray and set it aside.

Mix the flour, baking powder, ½ tsp of cinnamon, and ¼ cup of sugar in a bowl. In another bowl, whisk the milk, 2 tbsp of butter, and egg until smooth. Slowly, mix the dry mixture with the wet batter until smooth. Fill the donut pan holes with the batter three-fourths way full.

Bake for 10 minutes or until the donuts are lightly golden and spring back when pressed.

Mix the remaining sugar and cinnamon in a clean bowl. Transfer the ready donuts to a wire rack, brush them with butter, and roll them in the cinnamon sugar. Serve warm.

# 27. Key Lime Pie

Creamy, tangy, and excellently flavored pie with additional whipped cream topping for the sweet tooth.

**Prep Time: 20 mins**

**Cook Time: 25 mins**

**Chill Time: 1 hour**

**Serves: 8**

**Ingredients:**

- 1 ½ cups graham cracker crumbs
- ⅓ cup sugar
- 6 tbsp unsalted butter, melted
- 14 oz can of sweetened condensed milk
- ½ cup key lime juice
- 4 egg yolks
- 1 tsp grated lime zest
- 1 cup heavy cream
- 1 tbsp powdered sugar

**Instructions:**

Preheat the oven to 350°F.

Mix the graham cracker crumbs, sugar, and butter in a bowl. Press the mixture onto the bottom and sides of a 9-inch pie plate. Bake for 10 minutes or until lightly browned.

Whisk the condensed milk, lime juice, egg yolks, and lime zest until well combined. Pour the mixture into the crust. Bake for 15 minutes or until set. Cool for 10 minutes on your countertop and then in the refrigerator for at least 1 hour. Chill an empty bowl alongside.

Whip the heavy cream and powdered sugar in the chilled bowl until stiff peaks form.

Spread the whipped cream on the cooled pie before serving.

# 28. Strawberry Lemonade

Refreshing sweet lemonade speckled with fresh strawberries.

**Prep Time: 15 mins**

**Serves: 4**

**Ingredients:**

- 1 cup fresh lemon juice
- ½ cup sugar
- 4 cups cold water
- 1 cup fresh strawberries, hulled and sliced
- Ice cubes
- Fresh strawberries and lemon slices for garnish

**Instructions:**

Mix the lemon juice and sugar in a large pitcher until the sugar dissolves. Fill with the cold water and stir again.

Add the strawberries, stir gently, and add the ice.

Serve in glasses with ice cubes garnished with strawberries and lemon slices.

# 29. Chocolate Chip Cookie Skillet

Golden, warm, and gooey cookie skillet paired with vanilla ice cream.

**Prep Time: 10 mins**

**Cook Time: 25 mins**

**Serves: 4**

**Ingredients:**

- ½ cup unsalted butter, softened
- ½ cup brown sugar
- ½ cup granulated sugar
- 1 egg, cracked into a bowl
- 1 tsp vanilla extract
- 1 ½ cups all-purpose flour
- ½ tsp salt
- ½ tsp baking soda
- 1 cup semisweet chocolate chips
- Vanilla ice cream, for serving

**Instructions:**

Preheat the oven to 350°F. Grease a 9-inch cast iron skillet with cooking spray.

Cream the butter and both sugars in a large bowl with a hand mixer until light and fluffy. Add the egg and vanilla and beat until smooth.

Mix the flour, salt, and baking soda in a separate bowl and gradually mix it into the wet batter until well combined. Fold in the chocolate chips.

Spread the cookie dough in the skillet. Bake for 20 to 25 minutes or until golden brown and set.

Serve warm with dollops of vanilla ice cream.

# 30. Caramel Pie

No-fuss caramel pie using store-bought dulce de leche. Requires only 5 minutes and some patience for chilling.

**Prep Time: 15 mins**

**Cook Time: 5 mins**

**Chill Time: 4+ hours**

**Serves: 8**

**Ingredients:**

- 1 large egg, beaten
- 1 (9-inch) graham cracker crust
- 8 oz frozen whipped topping, thawed to room temperature
- 3 (13.4 oz) cans of dulce de leche
- For garnish:
- 1 cup canned whipped topping
- ¼ cup chopped pecans
- ¼ cup chocolate morsels

**Instructions:**

Preheat the oven to 375°F.

Brush the pie crust with the egg and bake for 5 minutes. Cool the crust completely before proceeding.

Whisk the whipped topping and dulce de leche in a bowl until smooth. Pour the mixture into the cooled pie crust and smoothen and flatten it out. Refrigerate for at least 4 hours.

When ready to serve, garnish with whipped topping, pecans, and chocolate morsels.

# Conclusion

Ready to upgrade your meal plan?

These recipes will surely bring on some excitement, new flavors, and options to it. Whether for individual or family servings, each recipe surely makes a good pass.

# Dear Reader

First and foremost, I would like to express my gratitude for downloading and reading my book. I hope that you found it informative and enjoyable. Writing books is my way of sharing my skills and expertise with readers like you.

I am aware that there are countless books available, and I am truly grateful that you chose mine. Your decision means a lot to me, and I am confident that you made the right choice.

If you could provide me with honest feedback about my book, it would make me even happier. Feedback is essential for growth and development. It helps me to improve the content of my book and generate new ideas for future publications. Who knows, your feedback might just spark an idea for my next book!

Thank you once again for taking the time to read my book, and I hope to hear from you soon.

*Sincerely,*

*Martin Beasant*

Made in the USA
Columbia, SC
06 April 2025